My First Day of Kindergarten Activity Book

My First Day of Kindergarten

activity book

55+

Games and Activities for What to Expect on Your Big Day

SARAH CHESWORTH

callisto
publishing
an imprint of Sourcebooks

For my family.

Published by Callisto Publishing LLC C/O Sourcebooks LLC
P.O. Box 4410, Naperville, Illinois 60567-4410
(630) 961-3900
callistopublishing.com

This product conforms to all applicable CPSC and CPSIA standards.

Source of Production: 1010 Printing Asia Limited, Kwun Tong, Hong Kong, China
Date of Production: December 2023
Run Number: 5034869

Printed and bound in China.
OGP 10 9 8 7 6 5 4 3 2 1

Contents

Note to Grown-Ups

I am excited you have chosen this book to help prepare your child for kindergarten! As a parent and former kindergarten teacher myself, I know how important this milestone is for your family.

The activities in this book are based on a typical kindergarten day, organized in chronological order. As your child completes the activities, they will discover some of the things they can expect on their first day, like getting ready for school and meeting new friends. Each page contains information to help start conversations about school, plus an activity with directions.

The activities incorporate kindergarten readiness skills such as colors, shapes, numbers, and letters. Each activity will build your child's confidence and get them excited about kindergarten. I encourage you and your child to take your time working through this book. Let your child set the pace to make sure that learning is a fun, positive experience.

I wish your child the most wonderful
year in kindergarten!

_____

is going to kindergarten!

Good Morning!

Search and Find

On your first day of kindergarten, it is important to wake up on time so you can get ready for school. Find and circle all the blue items in this bedroom.

How Are You Feeling?

Fine Motor

Draw a picture that shows how you're feeling about your first day of kindergarten.

Mixed-Up Clothes

Comparisons

Before you can go to kindergarten, you need to get dressed!
What will you wear on your first day of school? Circle the piece of
clothing that is different in each row.

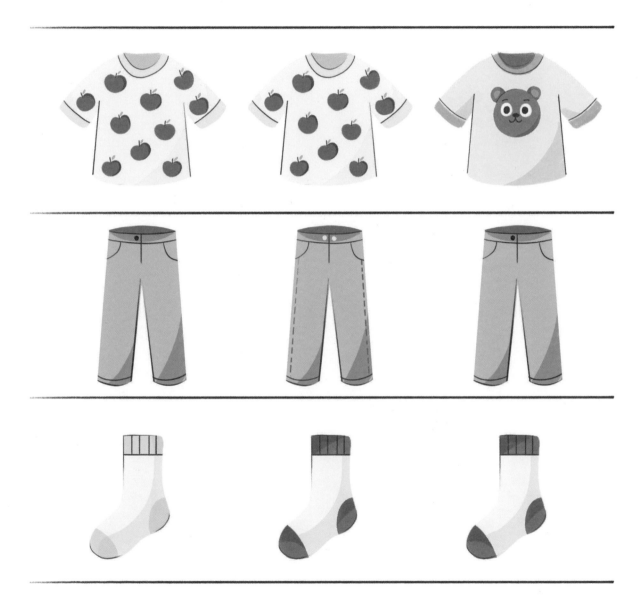

B Is for Breakfast

Writing

Eating a healthy breakfast helps your brain and body feel their best. Breakfast starts with the letter B. Trace and write the Bs below. Then follow the uppercase Bs to get to a healthy breakfast.

My First Day of Kindergarten Activity Book

Pack Your Backpack

Sorting

Your backpack will help you carry items to and from school each day. Circle all the items you need to put in your backpack for school.

Shoe Shuffle

Matching

Before you leave for school, you need to put on shoes. Which shoes should you wear? Draw a line to match the type of shoe you should wear for each type of weather.

My First Day of Kindergarten Activity Book

Let's Go to School!

There are different ways to get to kindergarten. You might ride the bus, walk, or travel in a car. Put a check in each box that shows a way to get to school.

Count the Buses

Counting

Riding a bus is one way to travel to school. Draw a line from each number to the correct group of buses.

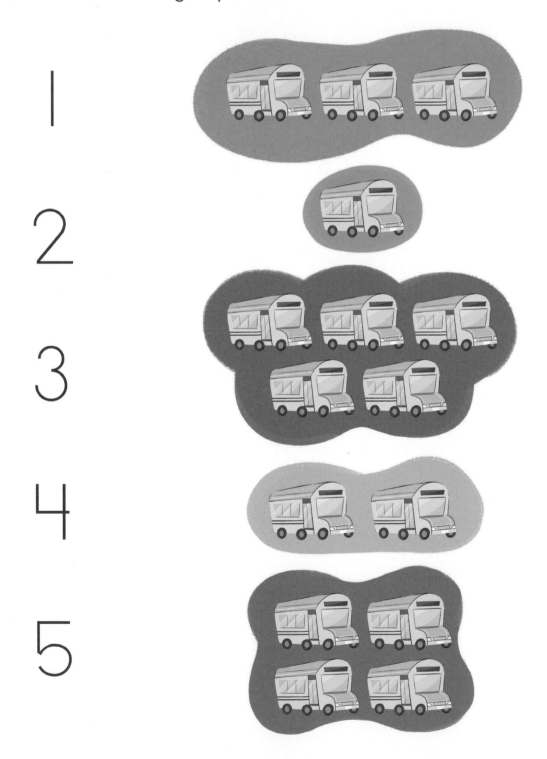

1

2

3

4

5

My First Day of Kindergarten Activity Book

School Shapes

School is a fun place for kids to learn. Every school looks a little different. Trace each shape in this school building, and then color it all in. Can you name each shape?

Which Classroom?

Fine Motor

There are many classrooms inside of school. Trace each path to help each kid find their classroom.

Counting Chairs

Counting

Your kindergarten classroom has tables and chairs that are just your size! Count and circle the chairs in this classroom. How many chairs are there?

What's On Teacher's Desk?

Search and Find

There are teachers at your school! Teachers love to help kids learn new things. Find and circle all the red items on the teacher's desk.

My First Day of Kindergarten Activity Book

Put Away the Backpacks

Matching

Your teacher will show where you can keep your backpack. Find out where these backpacks belong. Draw a line from each backpack to the hook with the matching lowercase letter.

Really Colorful Rug

Shapes

Your classroom might have a colorful rug to sit on. Let's get ready for circle time! Color the shapes on this classroom rug to match the shapes at the bottom of the page.

Green   Red   Blue

Raise Your Hand!

Counting

You will learn new rules in kindergarten. What should you do when you want to speak during class? Draw a line to connect the dots from 1 to 10 to find out!

Everything in Its Place

Comparisons

Everything in a classroom has its own special place. When you are finished playing with something, put it away. Circle the five things that are different in these pictures.

My First Day of Kindergarten Activity Book

Time to Share

Sorting

Because there are lots of kids at school, sometimes you have to share. Put a check in each box that shows an item at school you might need to share.

So Many Supplies!

It's important to take care of your school supplies, like your crayons, pencils, and scissors. Color each section with a circle (o) in yellow. What school supply do you see?

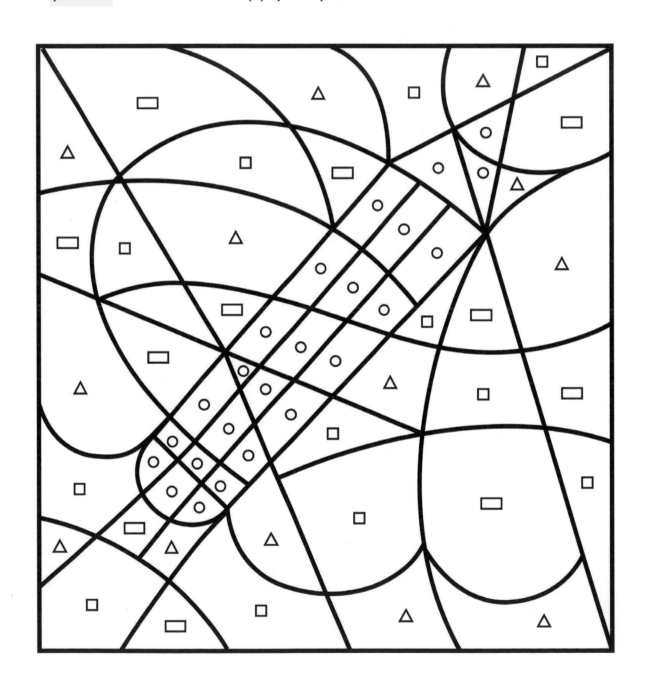

F Is for Friends

Writing

One very exciting thing about school is meeting new friends! Trace and write the Fs below. Then follow the uppercase Fs to find new friends.

New Friends

Patterns

Some of your new friends will look like you and some friends will look different from you! Circle the friend who comes next in each row.

My First Day of Kindergarten Activity Book

School Helpers

There are many adults to help you at school. School helpers have jobs like making lunch or helping you cross the street. Draw a line from each item to the school helper who uses it.

How Are You Feeling?

Draw a picture that shows you playing with your new friends from class.

You Can Help, Too!

Fine Motor

A janitor is a school helper who keeps the school clean. You can help, too! Help this kindergartner through the maze to throw out their trash.

Let's Trace Letters!

Learning to write letters is a fun part of kindergarten! Trace each uppercase and lowercase letter to practice.

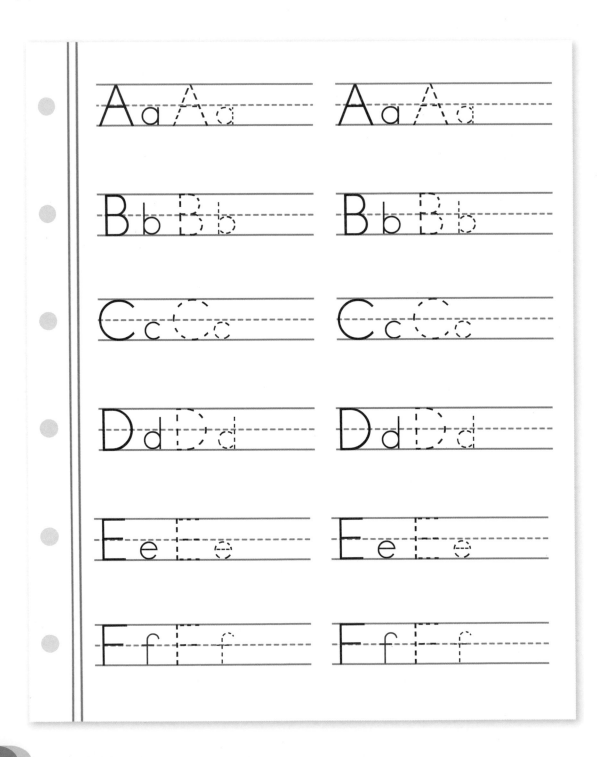

Let's Trace More Letters!

Learning to write letters is a fun part of kindergarten! Trace each uppercase and lowercase letter to practice.

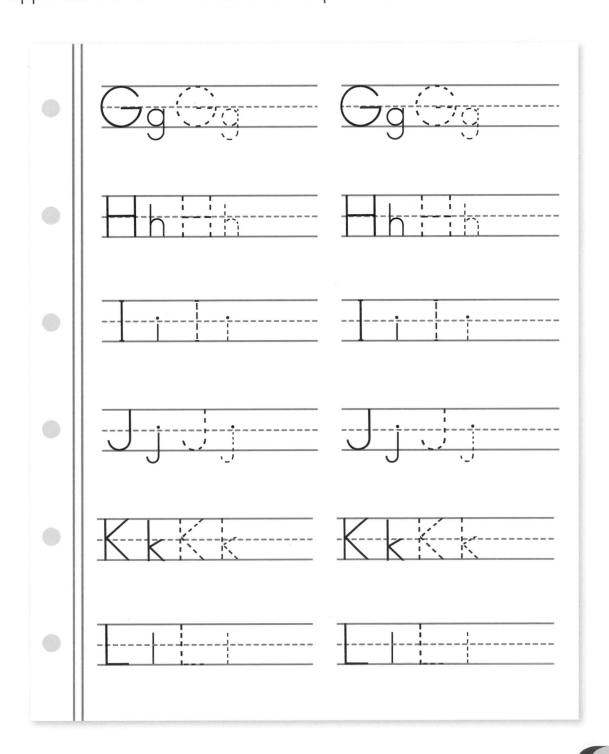

Letter Sounds

Writing

Each letter has a name and a sound. Trace each uppercase and lowercase letter while making the letter's sound.

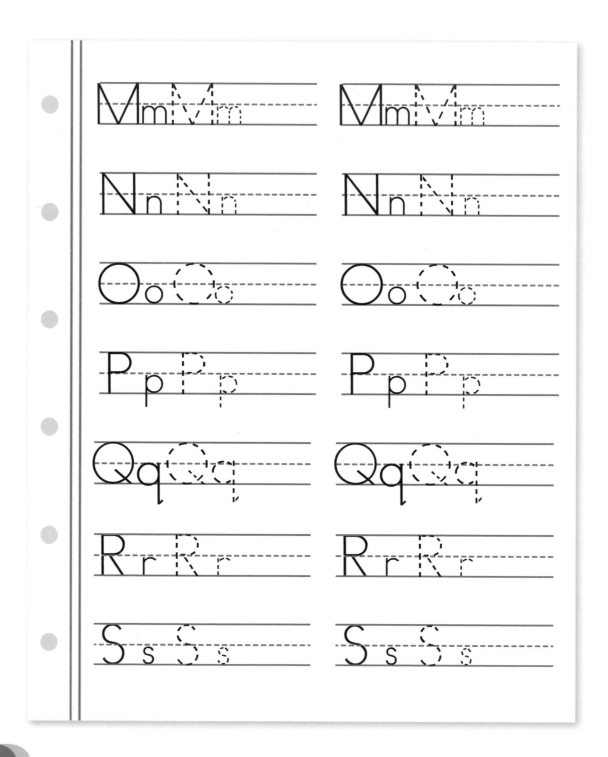

My First Day of Kindergarten Activity Book

More Letter Sounds

Writing

Each letter has a name and a sound. Trace each uppercase and lowercase letter while making the letter's sound.

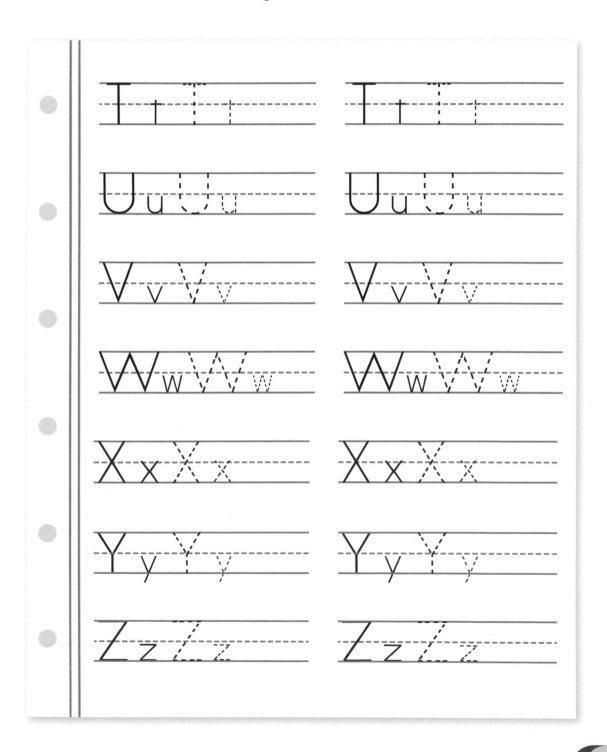

You're an Alphabet Star!

Letters

Singing "The Alphabet Song" can help you remember the order of the letters. Connect the dots from A to Z. Sing the song to help you! What did you draw?

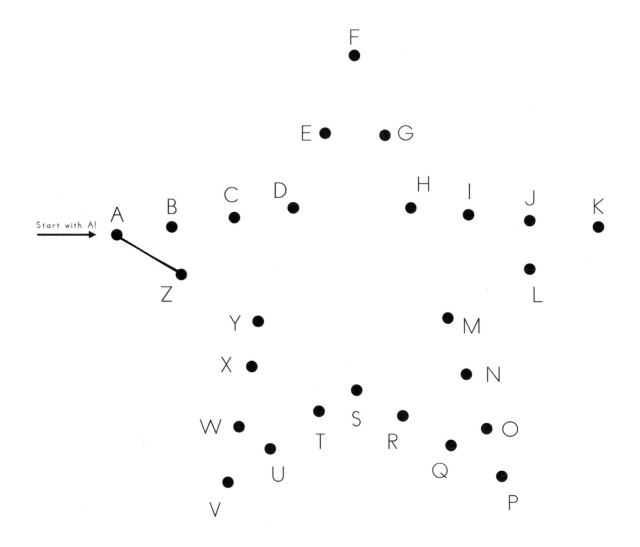

What's Your Name?

Your name is a special word that begins with an uppercase letter. Practice writing your name on the line and on each school item.

Count the Cubes!

Counting

Learning numbers is another fun part of kindergarten! Count the cubes in each tower and then trace the number at the top.

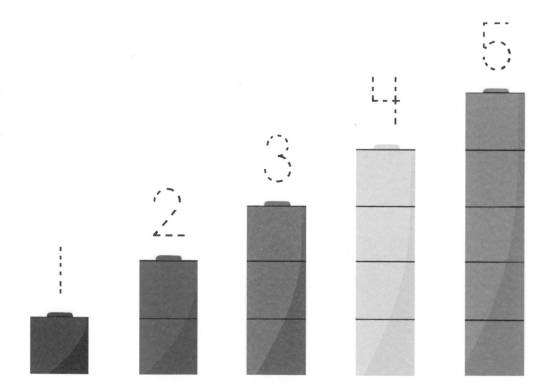

My First Day of Kindergarten Activity Book

Count Down

Counting

Do you know how to count backward? Count the cubes in each tower and then trace the number at the top. Now read the numbers from right to left. You are counting backward!

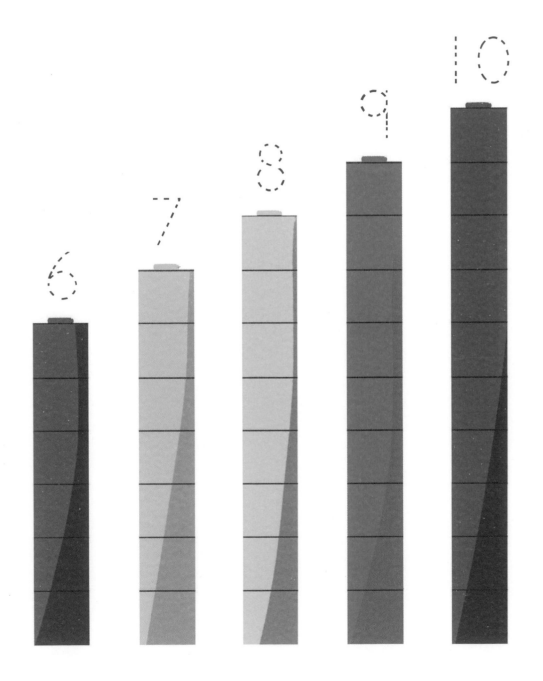

It's Story Time!

Comparisons

You will listen to and read many new books in kindergarten. Circle the five things that are different in these pictures of story time.

My First Day of Kindergarten Activity Book

Word Match

In kindergarten, you learn how to read words, too! Draw a line from each word to its matching word.

 c a t

 b u s

 d o g

 s u n

 b u s

c a t

 s u n

d o g

33

Lunchtime!

Patterns

At lunchtime, you eat with your friends. You can bring a lunch from home or eat one from the cafeteria. Circle the lunch food that comes next in each row.

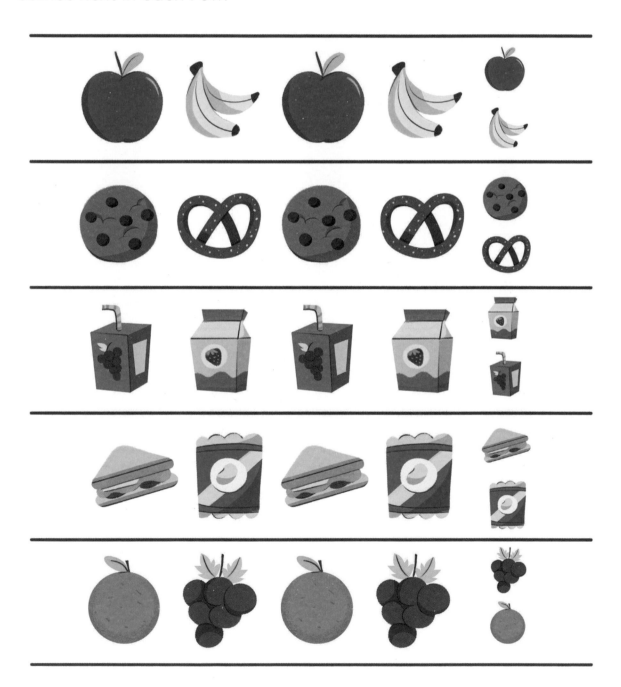

My First Day of Kindergarten Activity Book

L Is for Lunch

During lunchtime, you eat your food and quietly talk with your friends. Trace and write the Ls below. Then follow the uppercase Ls to get to the lunch table.

Time for Recess

Recess is when you can play with your friends on the playground. It's fun! Circle each number 4 that you find in this playground.

Down the Slide

Sequencing

During recess, you can climb, run, swing, and slide! How do you use the slide? Put the slide pictures in order by writing a 1, 2, or 3 in each box.

Bubble Pop

Writing

Washing your hands at school helps keep you healthy! Use soap and water to wash away germs. Trace and say each number in the bubbles while this kindergartner washes.

My First Day of Kindergarten Activity Book

Tissues to the Trash

Matching

If you need to sneeze at school, use a tissue. Tissues should always go into the trash. Draw a line from each tissue to the trash can with the matching lowercase letter.

Shape Patterns

Patterns

In kindergarten, you learn about shapes. What shapes do you know? Circle the shape that should come next in each row.

My First Day of Kindergarten Activity Book

S Is for Shapes

Tracing

Circles, squares, triangles, and rectangles are all different shapes. So are octagons and ovals. Trace and write the Ss below. Then carefully trace the shapes and color them in.

Crayon Box

Writing

You learn the names of colors in kindergarten! What colors do you already know? Trace each color word and then color the crayons to match.

Colors All Around

Writing

Do you have a favorite color? What things can you think of that are that color? Now that you've had some practice, trace these color words and color the crayons to match.

Class Pet

Colors

Your kindergarten classroom might have a class pet—or pet rocks! Put an X on all the red rocks, circle the purple rocks, and put a check mark on the yellow rocks.

My First Day of Kindergarten Activity Book

Listening to Others

Comparisons

It's important to listen when your teacher or other students are speaking. They listen to you, too! Circle the 5 things that are different in these pictures about show-and-tell.

Creation Station

Counting

Making art is a big part of kindergarten. Draw a line to connect the dots from 1 to 10 to see a place you can make art. Then draw a picture on it.

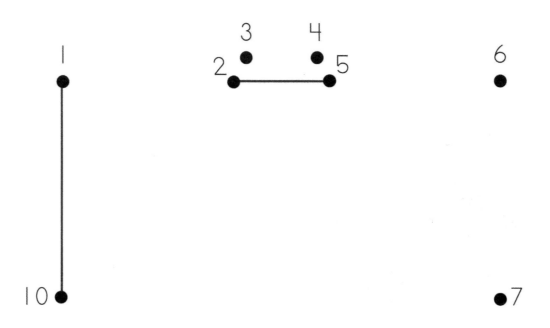

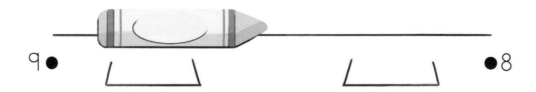

My First Day of Kindergarten Activity Book

Da-dum Drum

You might have a music class in kindergarten. Instruments are used to make music. Find and circle each of the musical instruments in the classroom.

piano guitar maracas drum tambourine

You Can Read!

Matching

Learning to read new words is an exciting part of kindergarten! Can you read the words **can** and **see**? Draw lines from each word at the bottom to all the matching words above it.

My First Day of Kindergarten Activity Book

Sunny Sight Words

Reading

Sight words are words that you learn to read just by looking at them. Read each sight word and use the code to color the picture.

Your Community

Comparisons

You learn about your community helpers in kindergarten. Your community helpers are people like firefighters, doctors, and mail carriers. Circle the community helper that is different in each row.

My First Day of Kindergarten Activity Book

Our World

Writing

In kindergarten, you learn more about the world. A globe is a model of the world that shows land and water. Trace the word and use the code to color the globe.

Science Match-Up

Matching

You learn about science in kindergarten. Science is how we understand how the world works. Draw a line to match the things you can study in science that go together.

My First Day of Kindergarten Activity Book

Is It Living?

Sorting

Part of science is learning about living things. Can you name something that is alive? Circle the things below that are alive.

Big Feelings

Reading

When you are at school, you might see people with many different feelings, like happy, sad, angry, or surprised. Draw a line from each feeling word to its matching word.

 happy

sad

 sad

surprised

 angry

happy

 surprised

angry

My First Day of Kindergarten Activity Book

Find the Feeling

Search and Find

You can sometimes tell how a person is feeling by looking at their face. Find and circle a person who is showing each of the feelings at the bottom of the page.

sad   happy   angry   surprised

Cleaning Up the Classroom

Numbers

At the end of a busy day of kindergarten, it will be time to clean up the classroom. Help these kids clean up by writing the missing numbers on the boxes.

My First Day of Kindergarten Activity Book

Say Goodbye!

Writing

At the end of the day, you can say goodbye to your new friends with a wave, hug, or high five. Trace the letters below to say, "Goodbye!" and color the picture.

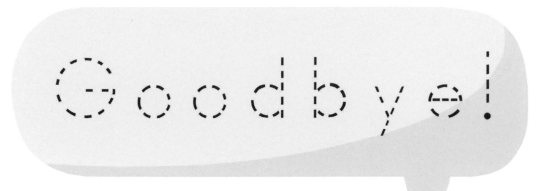

Time to Go Home

Shapes

After your fun day in kindergarten, it will be time to go back home. Color the path of squares to lead the bus home.

My First Day of Kindergarten Activity Book

K Is for Kindergarten

Writing

It was a great first day of kindergarten. You are excited for another day! Trace and write the Ks below. Then circle all the Ks you can find on the page. See you tomorrow!

How Are You Feeling?

Fine Motor

Draw a picture that shows how you feel now that you've completed your first day of kindergarten.

My First Day of Kindergarten Activity Book

Answer Key

Good Morning!

Mixed-Up Clothes

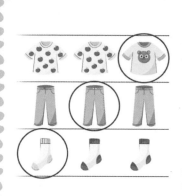

B Is for Breakfast

Pack Your Backpack

Shoe Shuffle

Let's Go to School!

Count the Buses

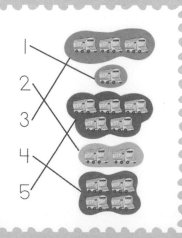

School Shapes
(Coloring may vary)

Which Classroom?

Counting Chairs
(5 chairs)

What's On
Teacher's Desk?

Put Away
the Backpacks

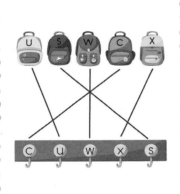

Really Colorful Rug

Raise Your Hand!

Everything in Its Place

Time to Share

So Many Supplies!
(A pencil)

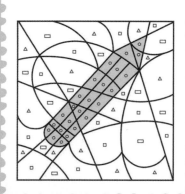

F Is for Friends

New Friends

School Helpers

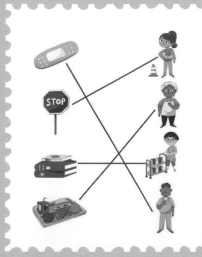

You Can Help, Too!

Let's Trace Letters!

AaAa AaAa
BbBb BbBb
CcCc CcCc
DdDd DdDd
EeEe EeEe
FfFf FfFf

Let's Trace More Letters!

GgGg GgGg
HhHh HhHh
IiIi IiIi
JjJj JjJj
KkKk KkKk
LlLl LlLl

Letter Sounds

MmMm MmMm
NnNn NnNn
OoOo OoOo
PpPp PpPp
QqQq QqQq
RrRr RrRr
SsSs SsSs

More Letter Sounds

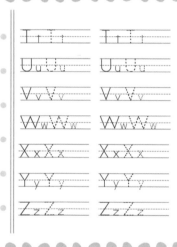

TtTt TtTt
UuUu UuUu
VvVv VvVv
WwWw WwWw
XxXx XxXx
YyYy YyYy
ZzZz ZzZz

You're an Alphabet Star!
(A star)

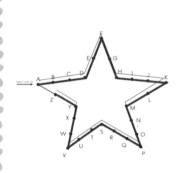

What's Your Name?
(Answers may vary)

My Name

My Name

Notes

My Name

Count the Cubes!

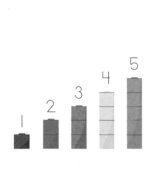

Count Down

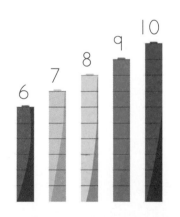

6 7 8 9 10

It's Story Time!

Word Match

Lunchtime!

L Is for Lunch

Time for Recess

Down the Slide

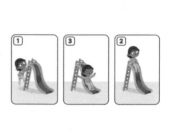

Bubble Pop

Tissues to the Trash

Shape Patterns

S Is for Shapes

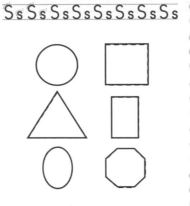

Crayon Box

Colors All Around

Class Pet

Listening to Others

Creation Station

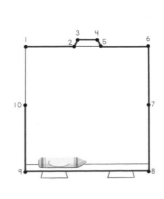

Answer Key

Da-dum Drum

You Can Read!

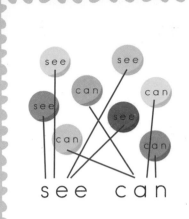

Sunny Sight Words

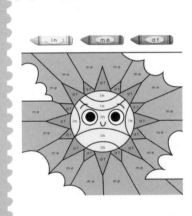

Your Community

Our World

Science Match-Up

Is It Living?

Big Feelings

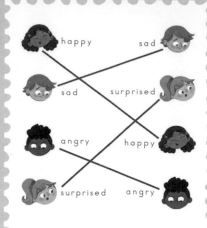

Find the Feeling

Cleaning Up the Classroom

Say Goodbye!
(Coloring may vary)

Time to Go Home

K Is for Kindergarten

Answer Key

Certificate of Completion

This certificate is presented to

for preparing for kindergarten!

Date _____

About the Author

Sarah Chesworth is a former kindergarten and first grade teacher. Now she spends her days teaching her own two little girls. She also helps busy parents and teachers make learning fun through her website and online teaching resources. She holds a bachelor's degree in early childhood education from Texas Tech University.